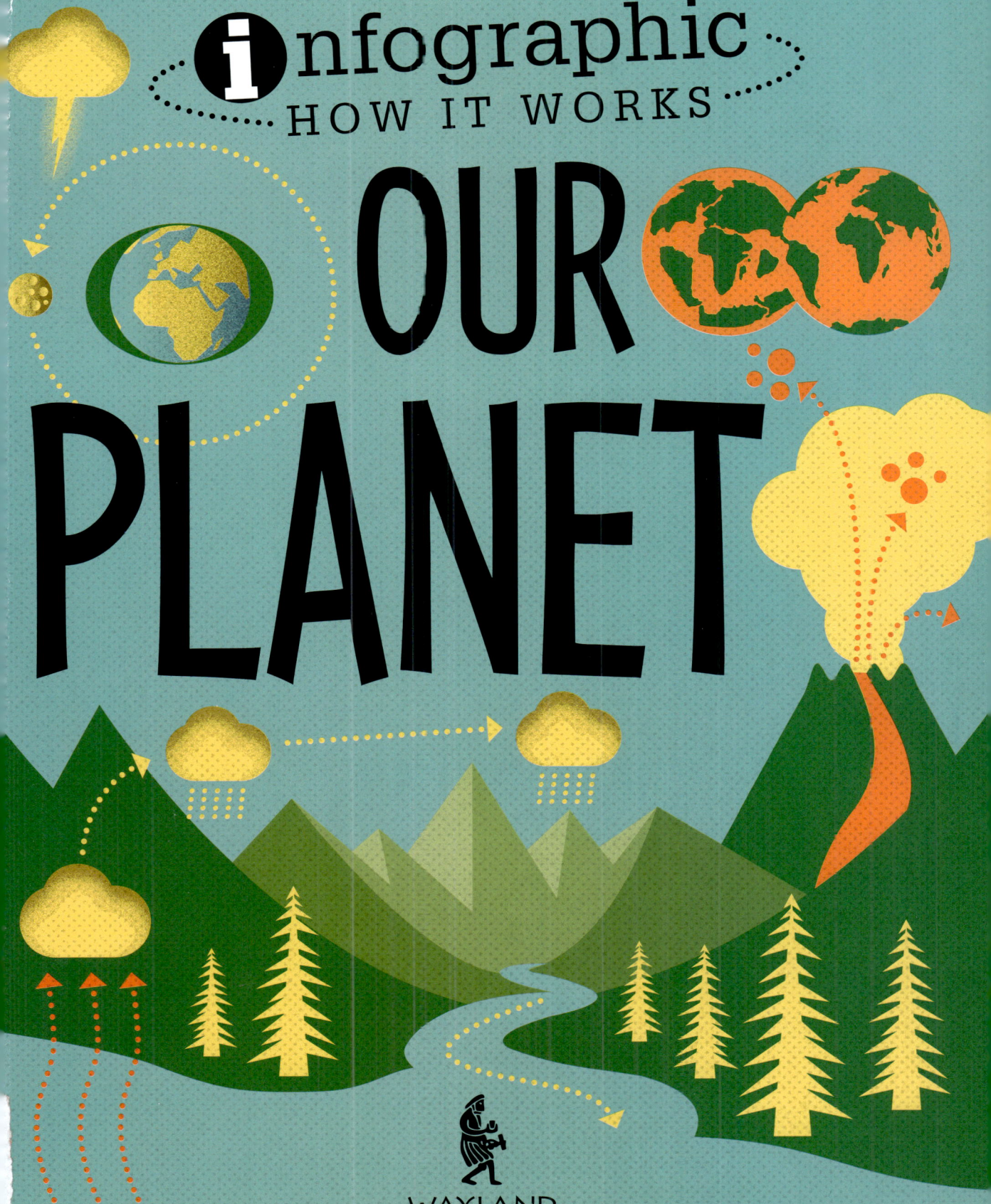

infographic
HOW IT WORKS

OUR PLANET

WAYLAND

CONTENTS

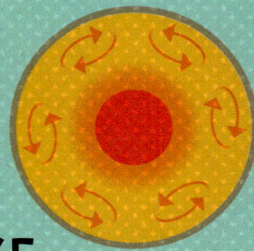

First published in Great Britain in 2016 by Wayland
Copyright © Wayland, 2016
All rights reserved

Editor: Liza Miller
Produced by Tall Tree Ltd
Editor: Jon Richards
Designer: Ed Simkins

ISBN: 978 0 7502 9930 5
10 9 8 7 6 5 4 3 2 1

MIX
Paper from responsible sources
FSC® C104740
FSC
www.fsc.org

Wayland
An imprint of Hachette
Children's Group
Part of Hodder and Stoughton
Carmelite House
50 Victoria Embankment
London EC4Y 0DZ

An Hachette UK Company
www.hachette.co.uk
www.hachettechildrens.co.uk

Printed and bound in China

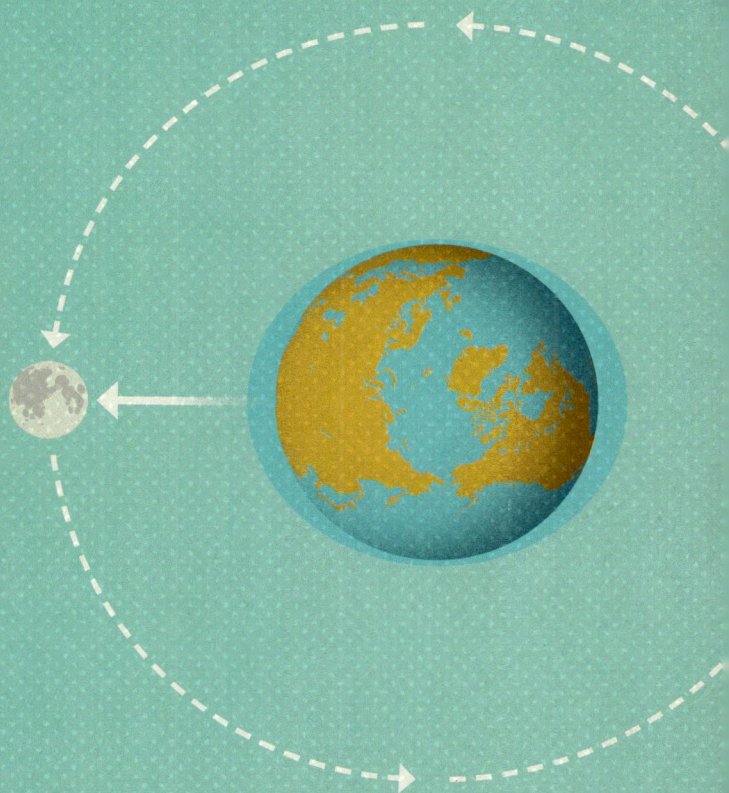

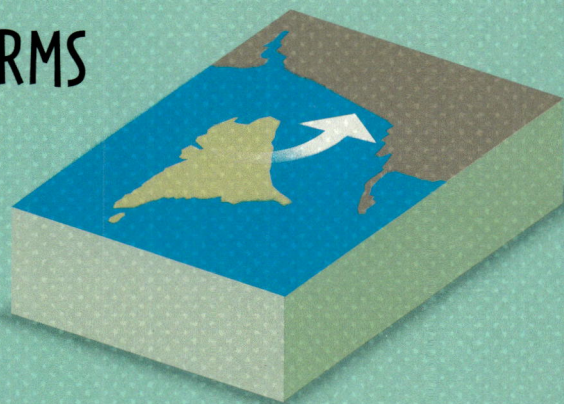

OUR
CHANGING PLANET

The surface of our planet is always on the move: towering peaks grow taller, volcanoes throw out liquid rock and rivers carve the landscape. This book will show you how these and other fantastic events occur, and what's really going on as they happen.

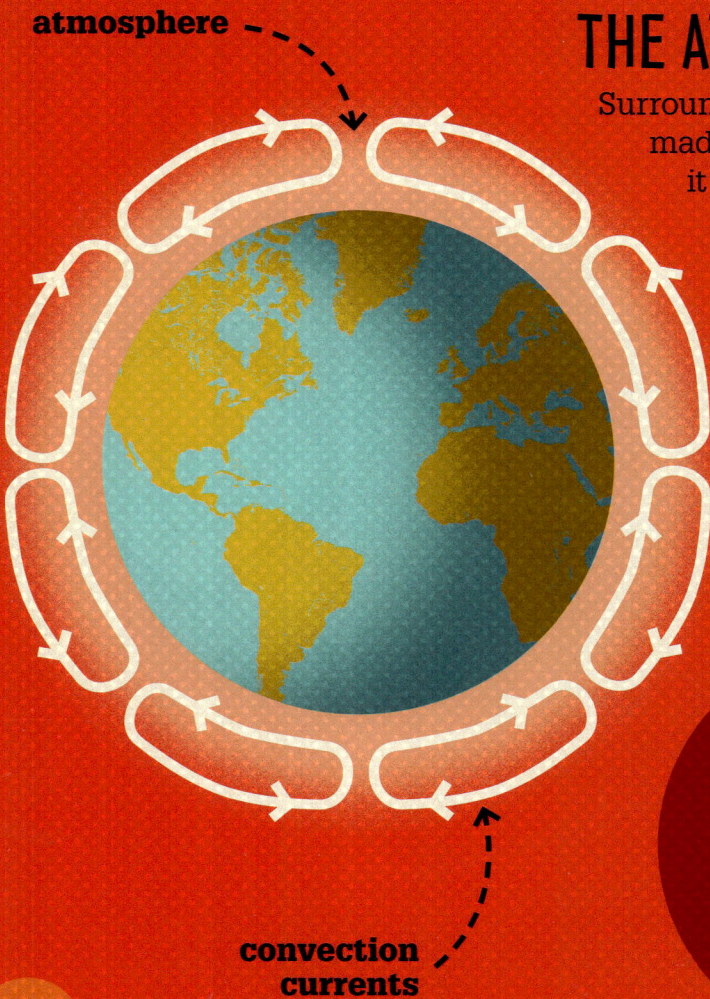

atmosphere

THE ATMOSPHERE

Surrounding our planet is the atmosphere, made up of different gases. Most of it consists of nitrogen, but about 20 per cent is oxygen, which is vital for all living things on Earth. Energy from the Sun heats the ground and this warms the gases above, causing them to swirl about in large patterns called convection currents. This movement of gases forms the basis of our weather.

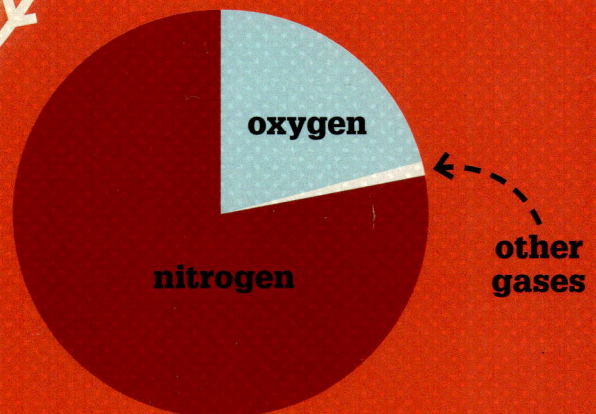

oxygen

nitrogen

other gases

convection currents

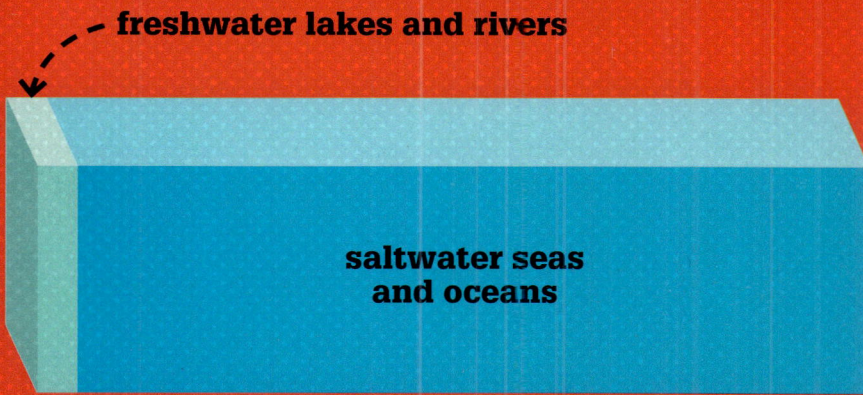

freshwater lakes and rivers

saltwater seas and oceans

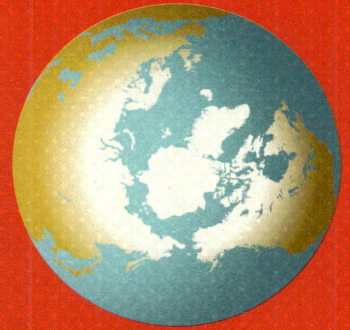

North Pole

OCEAN PLANET

More than 70 per cent of our planet's surface is covered with seas and oceans. Saltwater in the oceans makes up about 97 per cent of all the water on the planet. Freshwater makes up the remaining 3 per cent, and more than two-thirds of that is frozen solid in the glaciers and ice caps that surround Earth's poles.

South Pole

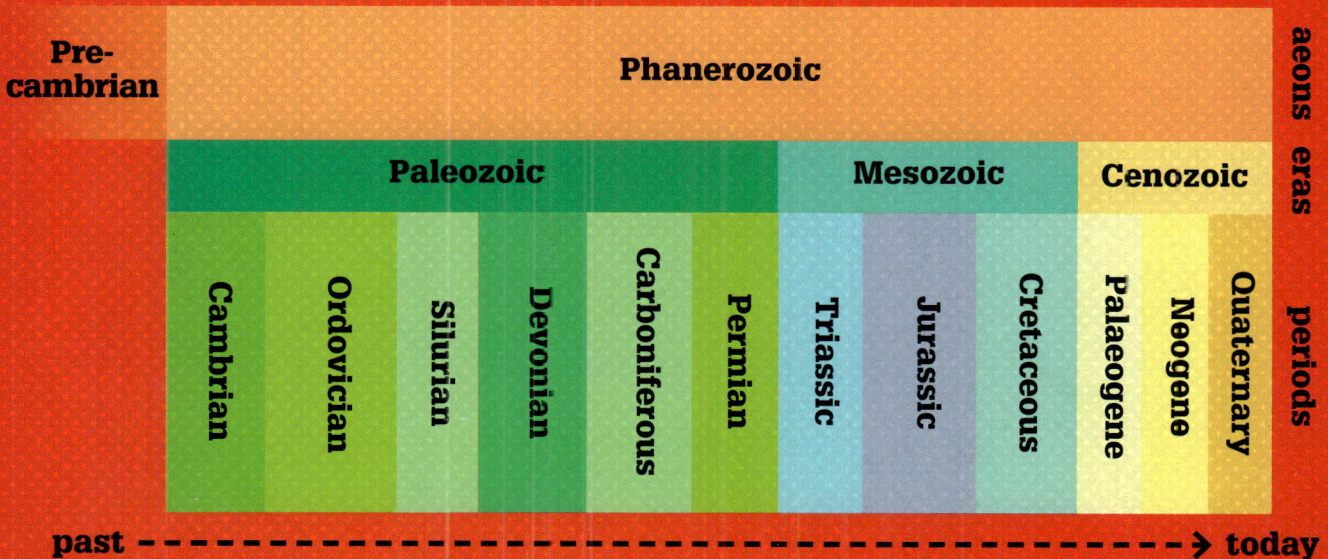

			aeons
Pre-cambrian	Phanerozoic		
	Paleozoic	Mesozoic	Cenozoic	eras
	Cambrian / Ordovician / Silurian / Devonian / Carboniferous / Permian	Triassic / Jurassic / Cretaceous	Palaeogene / Neogene / Quaternary	periods

past - → today

GEOLOGICAL TIME

Scientists break down the age of Earth into different sections, and these are split up into smaller units. The longest last for half a billion years or more and are called aeons. These are split into eras, which last several hundred million years. Eras are then sub-divided into periods, and these last for about 100 million years or less.

5

HOW EARTH WAS FORMED

About 4.5 billion years ago, Earth and all the other planets formed out of a swirling disc of gas, dust and rocks orbiting the young Sun. This early solar system was a violent place: asteroids, moons and comets slammed into each other.

① SWIRLING DISC

The cloud of gas, dust and rocks around the early Sun was called a protoplanetary disc.

② CLUMPS

Clumps of matter in the disc attracted more and more pieces of rock, forming small early planets.

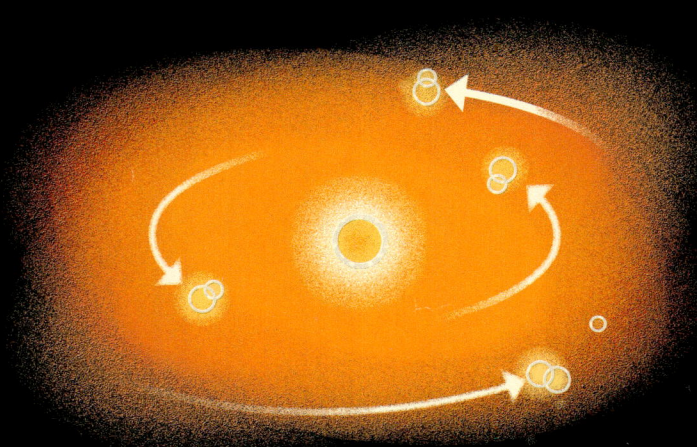

At some point in its early history, Earth was hit by a huge object about the same size as Mars. This collision threw up huge amounts of molten rock which clumped together to form our Moon.

❸ FORMING

The planets closer to the Sun were rocky and relatively small, while those further out were much bigger and made largely from ice and gases.

❹ SHINING STAR

More than 4 billion years ago, the early Sun started to shine. This explosion blew away much of the gas and dust, leaving behind the eight major planets and countless other bodies.

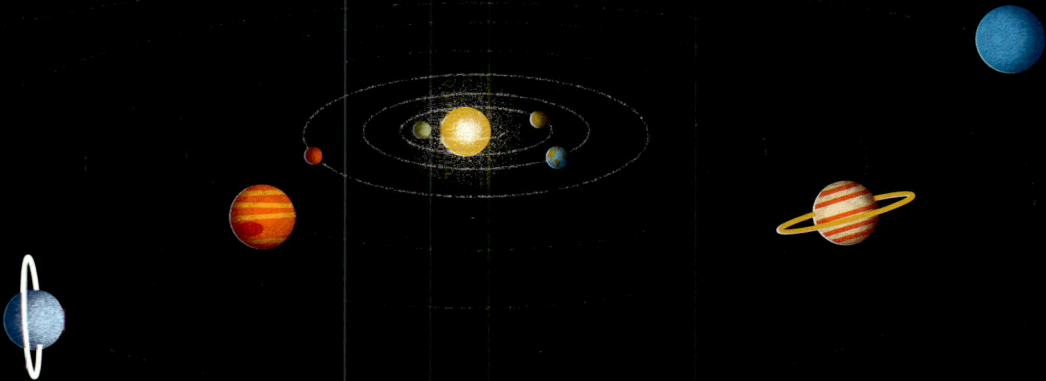

TRY THIS ...

The early Earth was bombarded by meteorites that covered its surface with craters for a time. Create your own craters by filling a small tray with sand and dropping marbles into it from different heights and angles.

HOW THE CONTINENTS MOVE

The interior of Earth is a mass of red-hot liquid rock which swirls about in huge currents. On top of all this is a thin layer of solid rock called the crust, which is pushed and pulled in all directions by the currents that move beneath it.

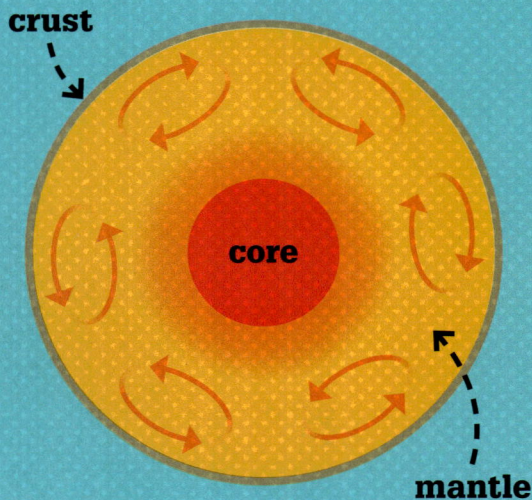

crust

core

mantle

tectonic plate

tectonic plate

currents

currents

1 INSIDE OUR EARTH

The layer below the crust is called the mantle. This is where the currents of molten rock occur.

2 PUSH AND PULL

The swirling currents push and pull on Earth's crust, cracking it into huge sheets of rock called tectonic plates.

3 FLOATING PLATES

Floating on the mantle, these tectonic plates move about very slowly. Over millions of years, they have changed how the surface of our planet appears.

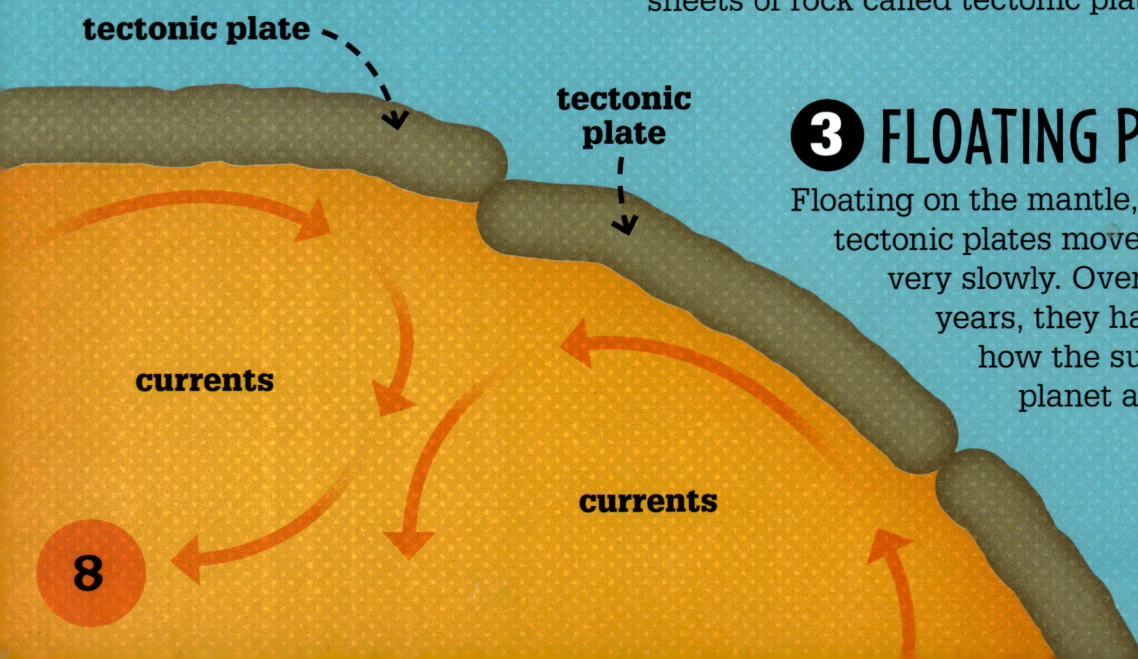

4 SUPERCONTINENT

About 300 million years ago, the areas of land carried by the tectonic plates were joined together to form one huge supercontinent, known as Pangaea.

Pangaea

5 SPLITTING UP

About 200 million years ago, Pangaea split apart into smaller pieces as the tectonic plates moved about.

200 million years ago

Earth's tectonic plates today

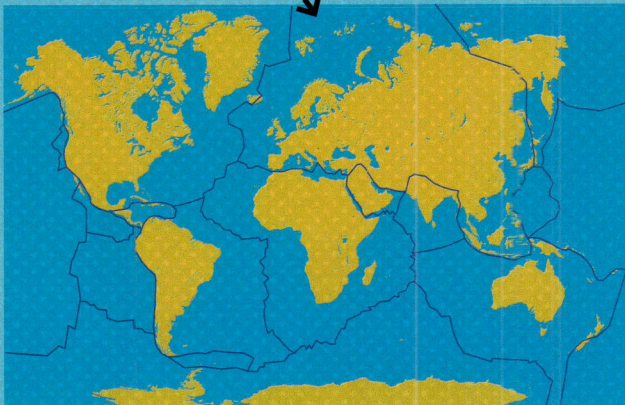

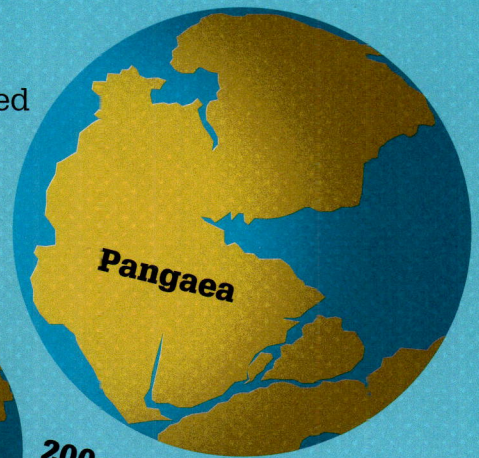

65 million years ago

6 OUR EARTH TODAY

The continents moved around on the tectonic plates over the next 200 million years, until they were in the positions they are today – but they are still on the move!

Today

TRY THIS ...

Find a map of Earth's tectonic plates and compare it to other maps showing where earthquakes and volcanic eruptions happen. Do you notice any similarities?

HOW AN EARTHQUAKE HAPPENS

Earth's tectonic plates don't always move smoothly. Sometimes they jar or get stuck, resulting in a build-up of energy, which is released in a sudden, powerful movement called an earthquake.

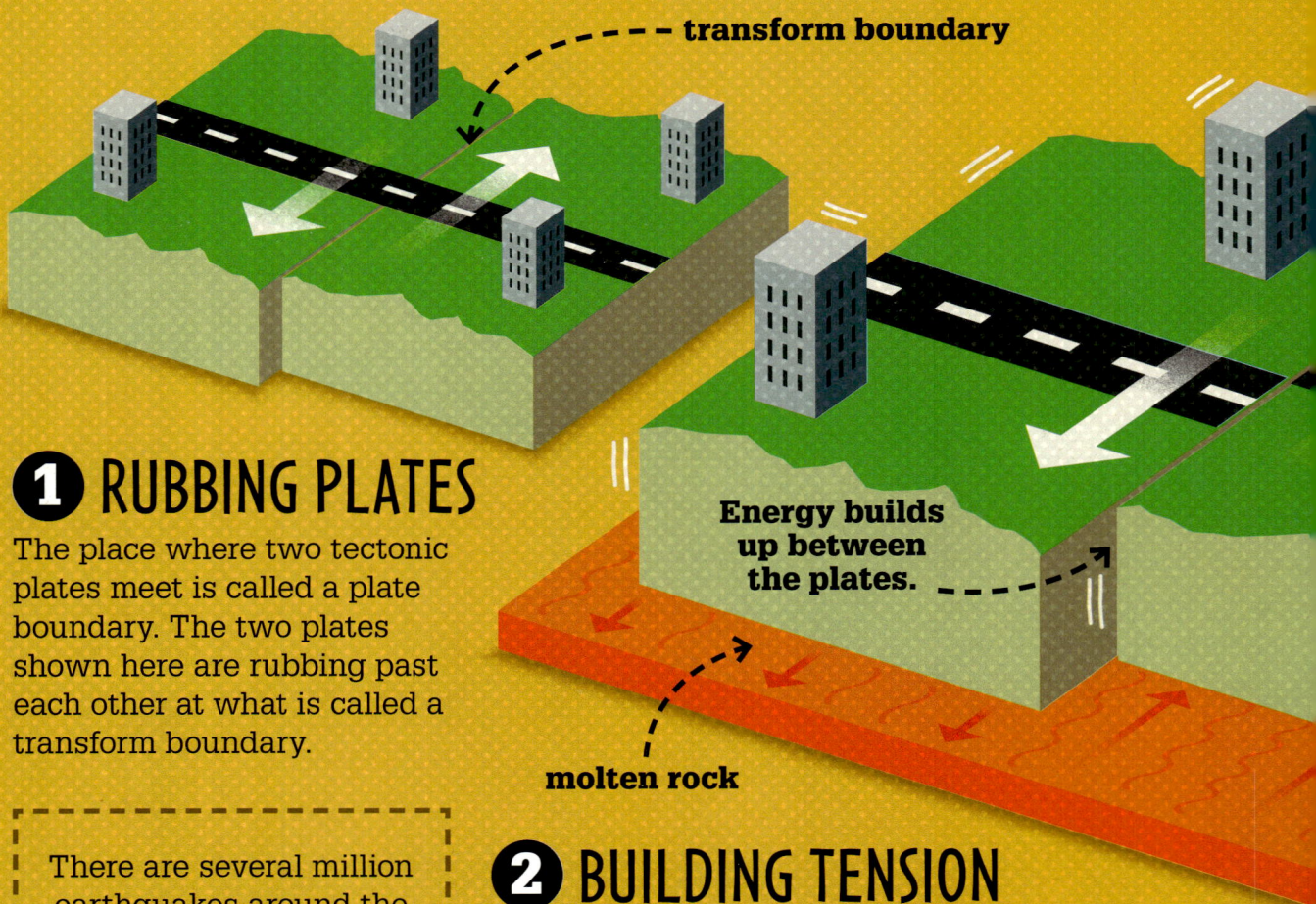

transform boundary

Energy builds up between the plates.

molten rock

1 RUBBING PLATES

The place where two tectonic plates meet is called a plate boundary. The two plates shown here are rubbing past each other at what is called a transform boundary.

There are several million earthquakes around the world every year, but most of them are too weak for us to notice.

2 BUILDING TENSION

Sometimes, the jagged edges of the plates become stuck, but forces from the swirling molten rock below continue to push and pull on the plates. This causes tension and energy to build up between the two plates.

Use two blocks of wood to represent tectonic plates. First wrap them in rough sandpaper and rub them together, then use smooth sandpaper and do the same. Is it easier to move the blocks when their sides are rough or smooth?

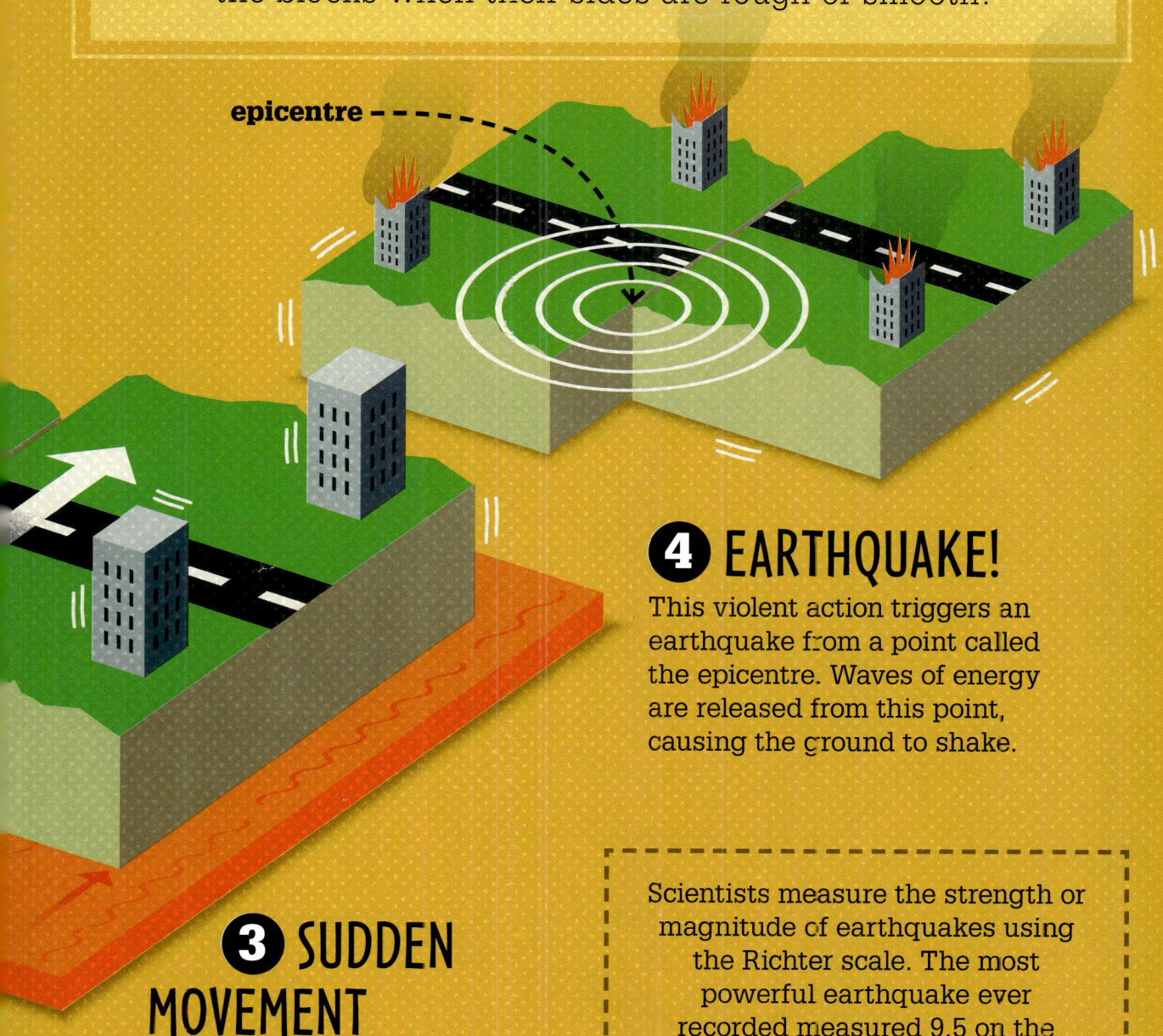

epicentre

4 EARTHQUAKE!

This violent action triggers an earthquake from a point called the epicentre. Waves of energy are released from this point, causing the ground to shake.

3 SUDDEN MOVEMENT

When this energy becomes too great, the plates are forced to move in an incredibly violent action.

Scientists measure the strength or magnitude of earthquakes using the Richter scale. The most powerful earthquake ever recorded measured 9.5 on the Richter scale. It occurred in Valdivia, Chile, in 1960.

11

HOW TO BUILD A VOLCANO

As the planet's tectonic plates move about, they create cracks and fractures through which molten rock, called lava, erupts, forming a volcano. Volcanoes come in many different shapes and sizes, depending on where they erupt and what exactly pours out of them.

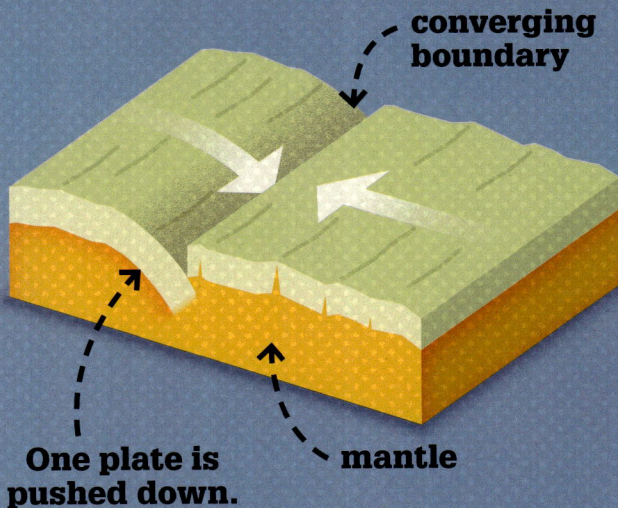

converging boundary

1 CRASHING PLATES

These two tectonic plates are crashing into each other, and one of them is being pushed down into the mantle. This plate boundary is called a convergent boundary.

One plate is pushed down.

mantle

2 SINKING

As the tectonic plate sinks into the mantle, its rock melts and rises up, pushing through the crust above it.

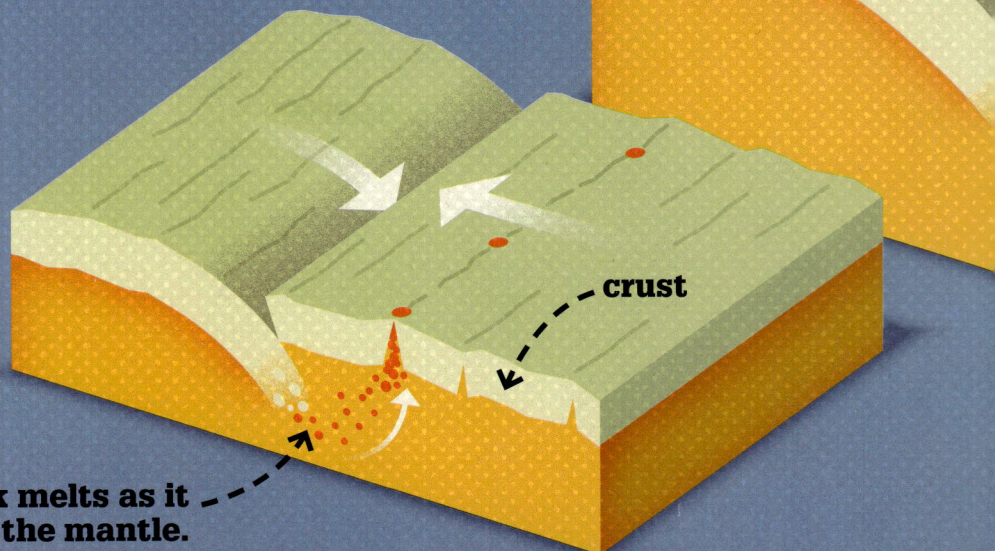

crust

The rock melts as it sinks into the mantle.

Make your own volcano by placing a small glass jar on a tray and filling it halfway with a mixture of water, washing-up liquid and vinegar. Add some red food colouring and then pour in two tablespoons of baking soda in one go. Watch as the mixture erupts!

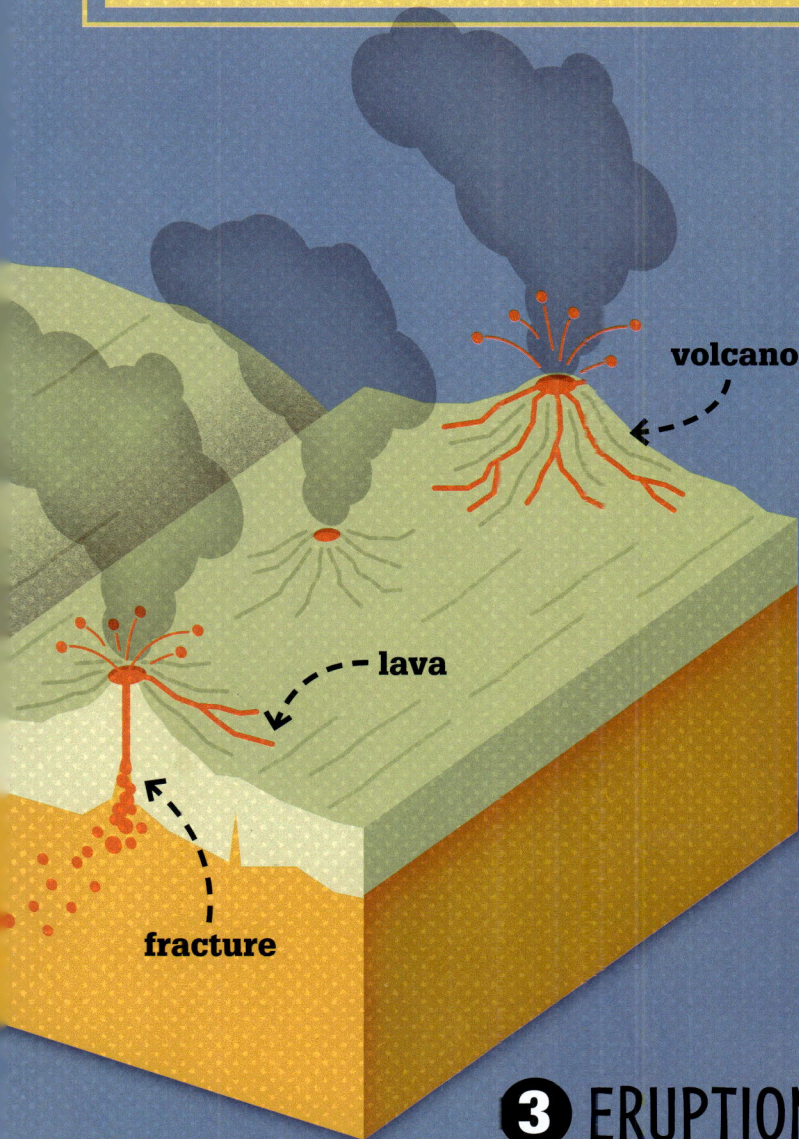

volcano

lava

fracture

❸ ERUPTION

When the liquid rock pushes up through the crust, it erupts on to the surface, creating volcanoes.

Composite

Shield

Dome

The shape of a volcano depends on what comes out of its opening, or vent. Composite volcanoes have steep sides and are formed from layers of ash and lava. Shield volcanoes have shallow, sloping sides that were formed by runny lava. Dome volcanoes have steep, domed sides that were formed by thick lava.

HOW TO MAKE MOUNTAINS

The crashing and bashing of Earth's tectonic plates as they move about create incredible features, such as huge valleys and towering peaks. Because the plates keep moving, these mountains and valleys gradually change shape and size.

1 MOVING PLATES

The Himalayas were formed when the Indian tectonic plate moved north and collided with the Eurasian tectonic plate.

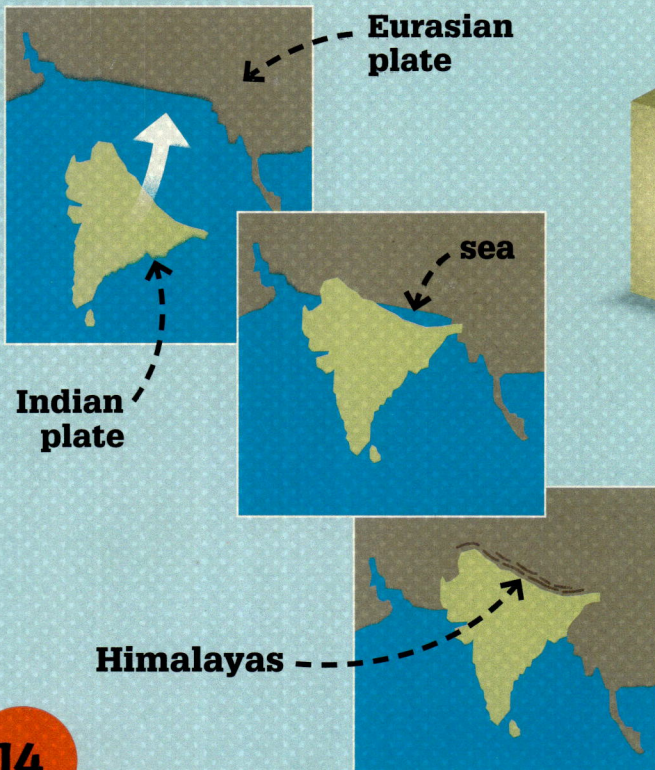

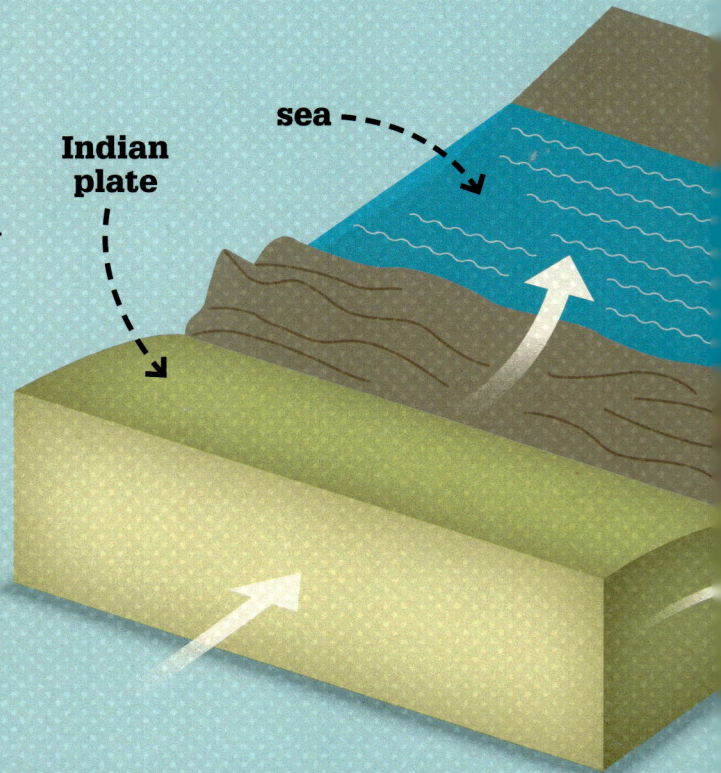

Eurasian plate

Indian plate

sea

Indian plate

sea

2 PUSHING UP

As the Indian plate moved north, it pushed up rock between the two plates, forcing out the sea between the two landmasses.

Himalayas

14

If the Himalayas are growing 7.5 mm every year, how much taller will they be in metres after 2,000 years?

The Himalayas have the highest mountain peaks in the world, including the tallest, Mount Everest. Its peak is at an altitude of 8,848 m.

Eurasian plate

❸ TOWERING PEAKS

Over millions of years, as the Indian plate continued to move north, it forced up any rock between the two plates, creating the towering peaks of the Himalayas.

Himalayas

The rock between the plates is forced up.

HOW ROCKS ARE FORMED

There are three types of rock: igneous, which comes from volcanic activity; sedimentary, which is formed by the action of water; and metamorphic, which is rock that has been changed by great heat and pressure.

1 THE ROCK CYCLE

Rocks are formed, destroyed and remade all the time, changing from one type of rock to another, in a process called the rock cycle.

Rocks and minerals are graded by their hardness. Talc, which is used to make talcum powder, is the softest mineral, while diamond is the hardest. Diamond is formed by enormous pressure and heat deep in the Earth's crust. It is brought to the surface by volcanic activity.

Talc

Diamond

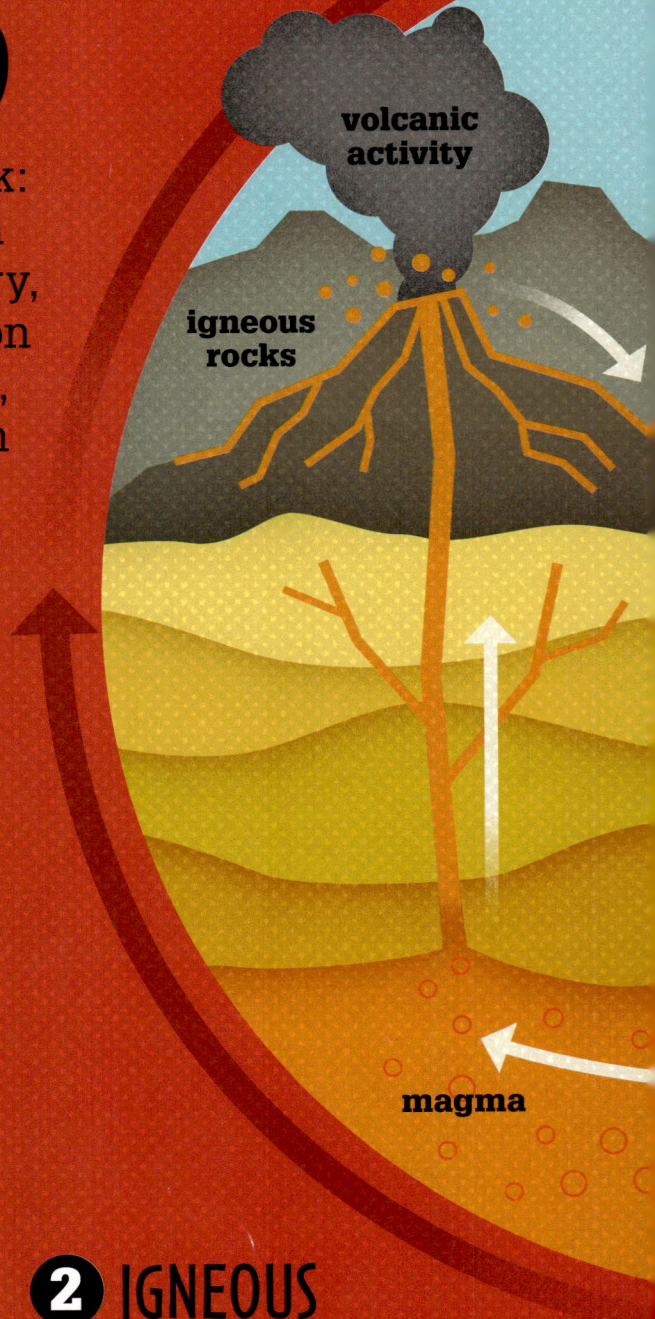

volcanic activity

igneous rocks

magma

2 IGNEOUS

Inside Earth, rock is a red-hot liquid called magma. Volcanic activity pushes this magma towards the surface where it cools to form igneous rocks.

3 WEATHERING

Over millions of years, these igneous rocks are weathered and eroded, breaking up into tiny particles such as sand and clay.

4 SEDIMENTARY

The particles are carried away by rivers and laid down in layer upon layer. The lower layers are squeezed together to form sedimentary rocks.

5 METAMORPHIC

The movements of tectonic plates squeeze and push the rocks, putting them under great heat and pressure. This changes them into metamorphic rocks.

6 MELTING

Further tectonic activity may push the rocks back down into the mantle, where they are melted back into magma.

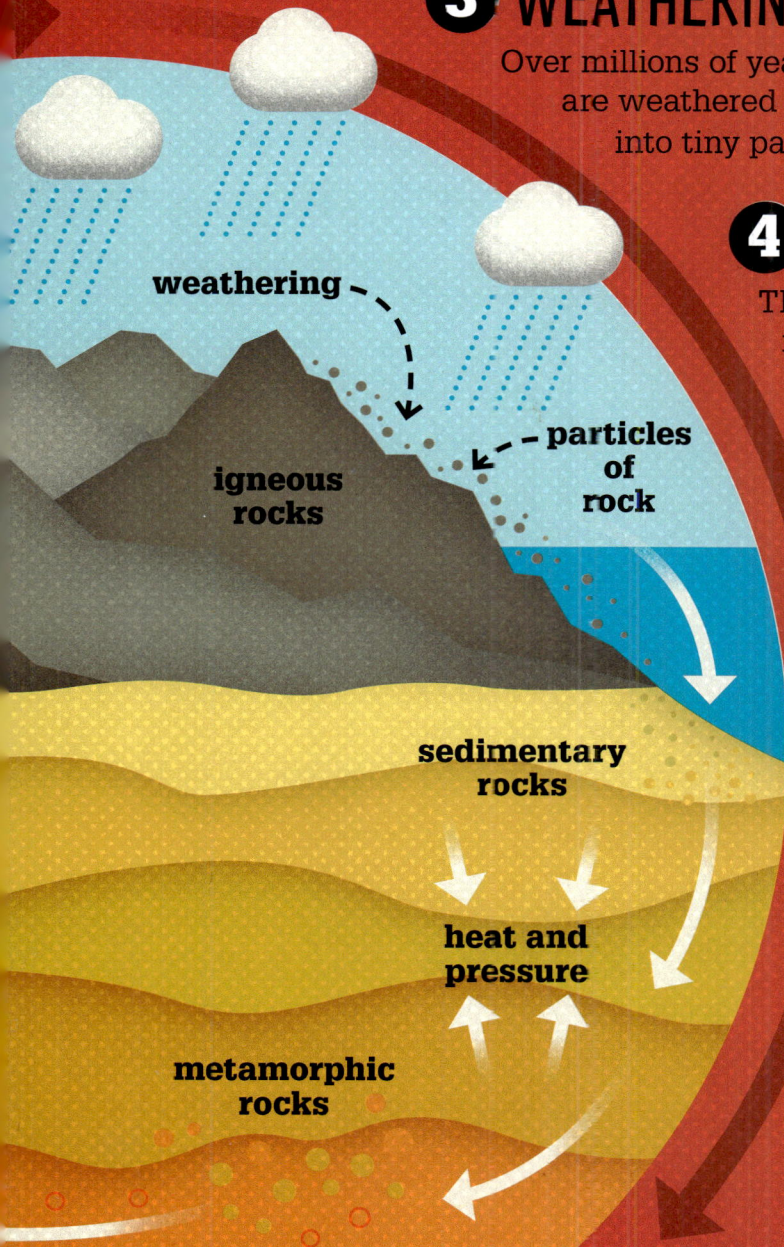

weathering

particles of rock

igneous rocks

sedimentary rocks

heat and pressure

metamorphic rocks

TRY THIS ...

Start your own rock collection by keeping interesting and unusual stones and rocks from your travels. See if you can identify what type of rock they are and how they may have been formed.

HOW TIDES WORK

Every object in the universe has an attractive force that pulls other objects towards it. This force is known as gravity. As well as keeping the planets in orbit around the Sun, and the Moon around Earth, this force also has an effect on Earth's oceans, making them rise and fall each day.

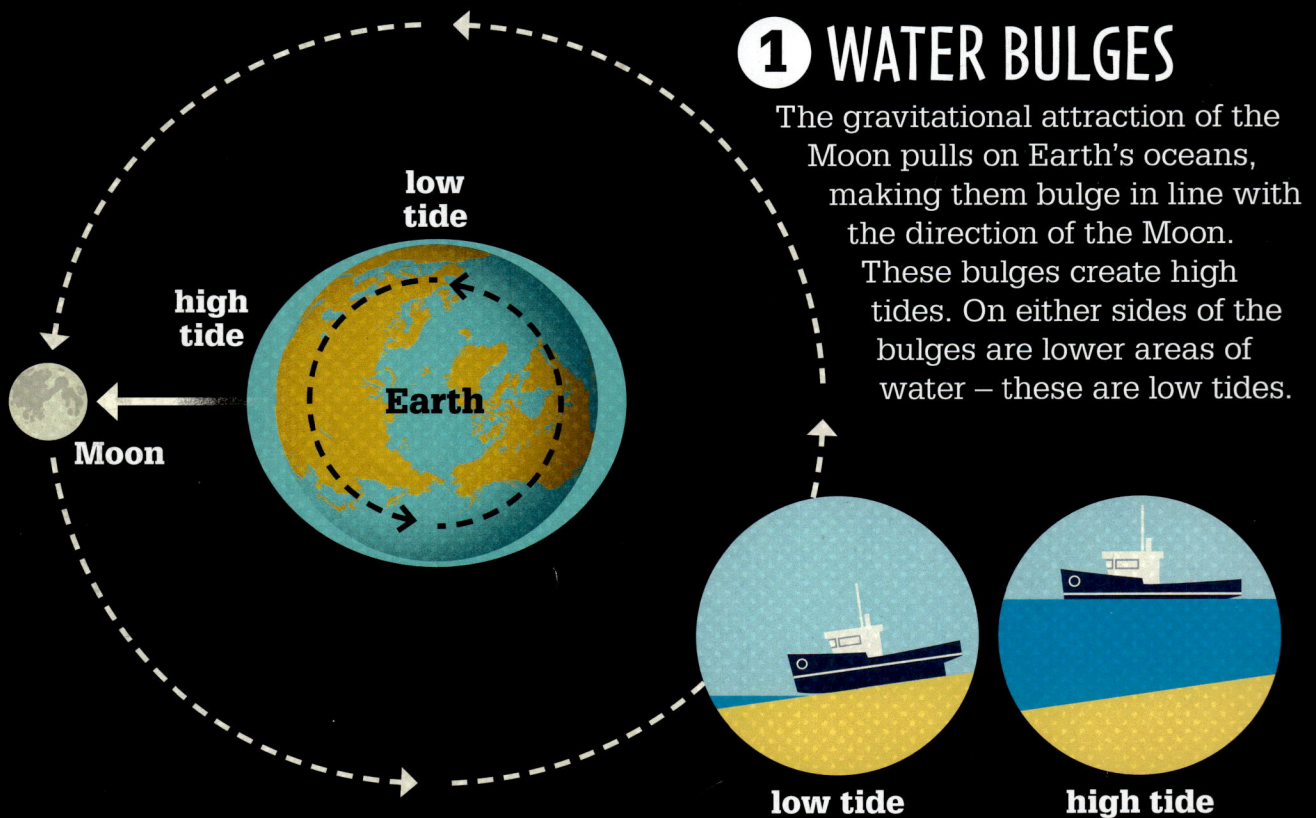

low
tide

high
tide

Earth

Moon

❶ WATER BULGES

The gravitational attraction of the Moon pulls on Earth's oceans, making them bulge in line with the direction of the Moon. These bulges create high tides. On either sides of the bulges are lower areas of water – these are low tides.

low tide

high tide

❷ HIGH TIDES

As Earth rotates, the bulges remain pointing in line with the Moon. Many parts of the planet will experience two high tides every day, since Earth spins round once every 24 hours.

③ SPRING TIDE

The Sun also has an effect on Earth's oceans, making them bulge towards it as well as the Moon. When the Sun and the Moon line up, they make the oceans bulge even more, creating a very high tide known as a spring tide.

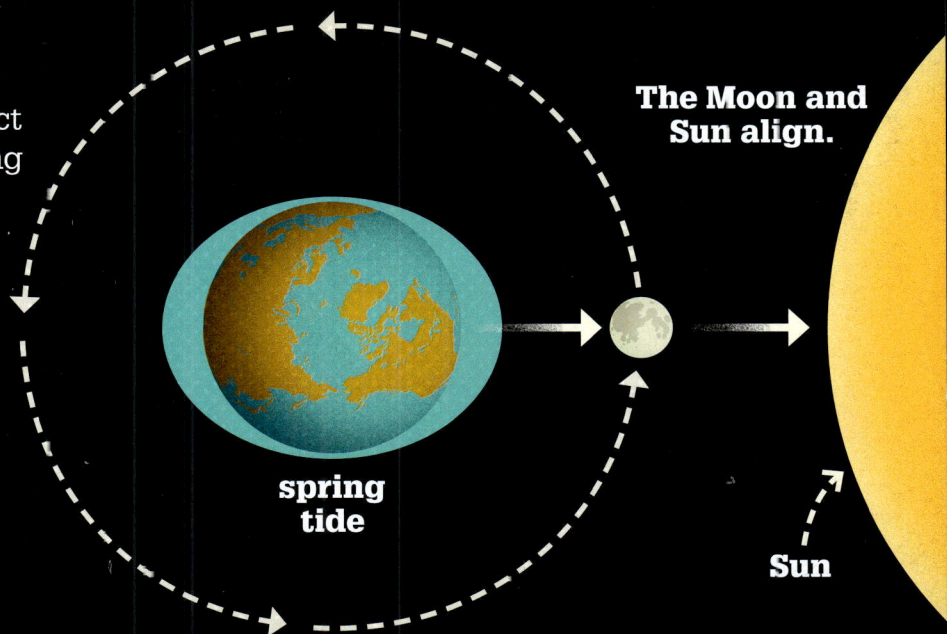

The Moon and Sun align.

spring
tide

Sun

④ NEAP TIDE

When the Sun and Moon are at right angles to each other, they create a very low tide, known as a neap tide.

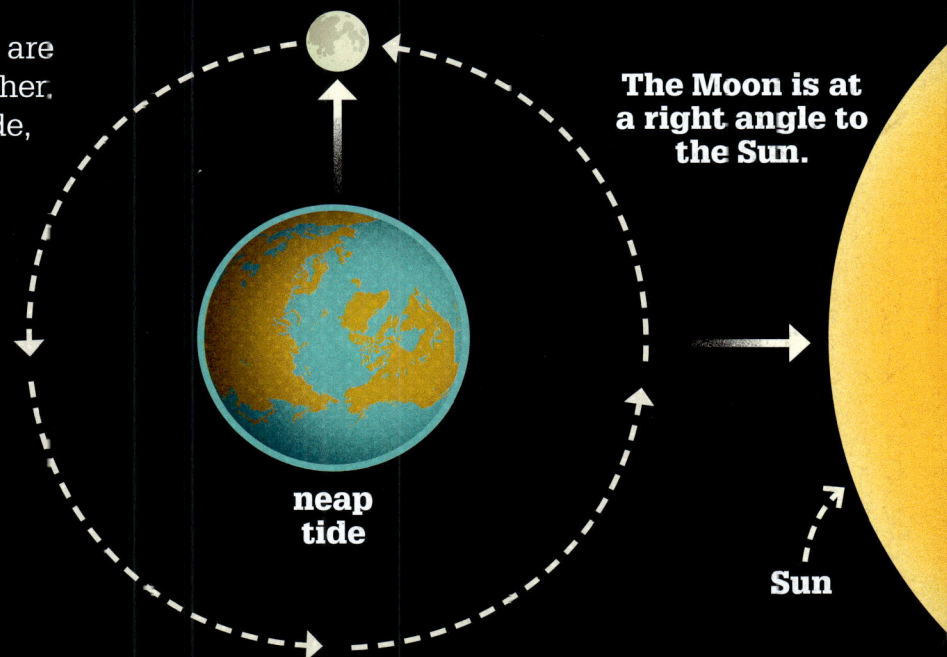

The Moon is at a right angle to the Sun.

The greatest tidal range on Earth occurs at the Bay of Fundy in Canada. The sea rises and falls by up to 16 m – as tall as a three-storey house!

neap
tide

Sun

TRY THIS ...

The Moon orbits Earth once every 28 days. If neap tides happen twice in each cycle, can you work out how far apart one is from the next?

19

HOW A RIVER CARVES A GORGE

Powerful rivers erode and alter the surrounding landscape. Under the right conditions they can create amazing features, including roaring waterfalls and spectacular steep-sided valleys called gorges.

1 ERODING

As a stream or river flows downhill, it erodes the rock on its banks and carries the debris away.

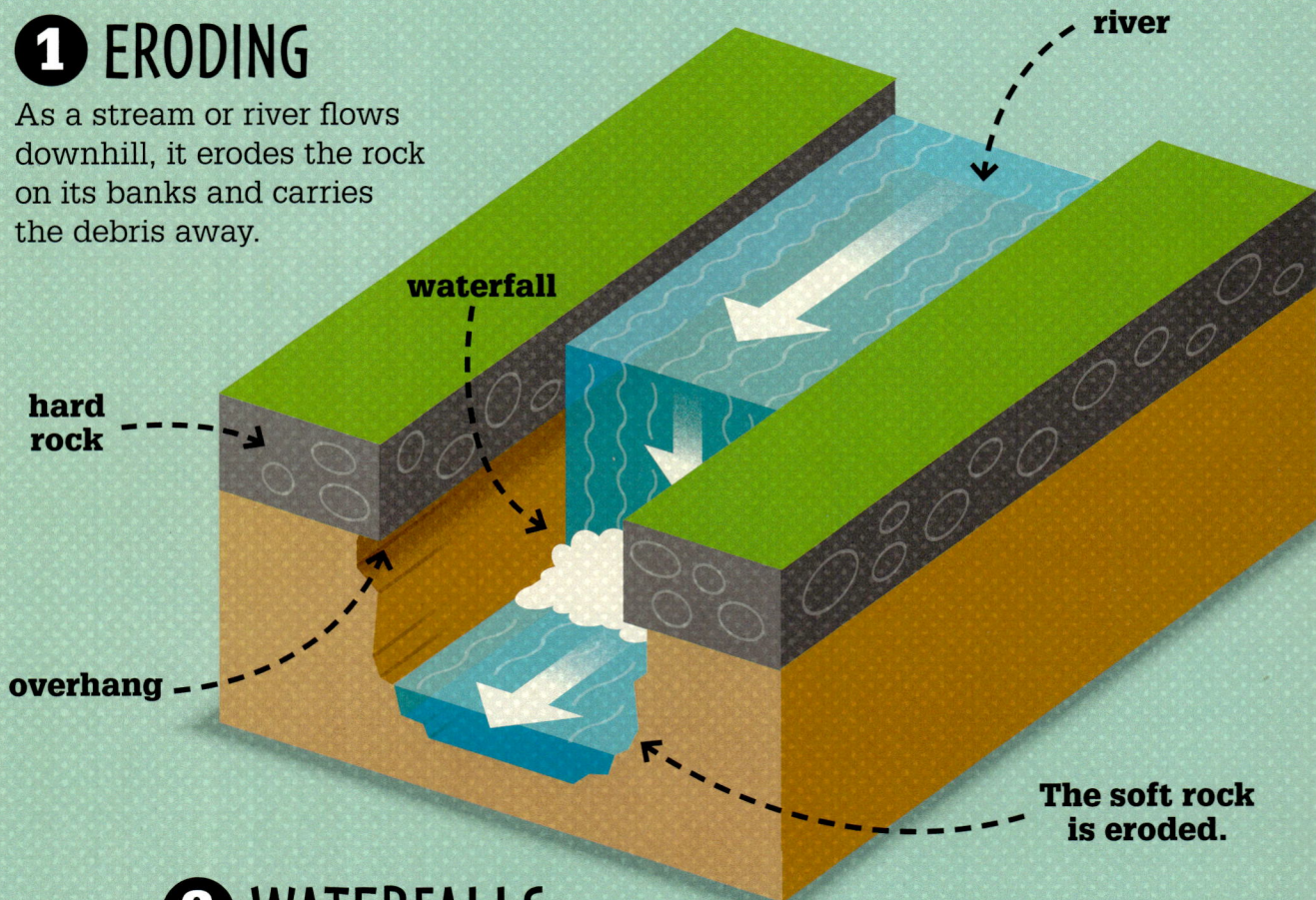

river

waterfall

hard rock

overhang

The soft rock is eroded.

2 WATERFALLS

A sudden drop in the course of a river is called a waterfall. As the water plunges over the lip of the waterfall, it erodes the softer rock beneath. This creates an overhang of harder rock. When the overhang becomes too large, it will not be able to support itself and will collapse.

Carved by the Colorado River, the Grand Canyon is nearly 450 km long, up to 30 km wide and almost 2 km deep.

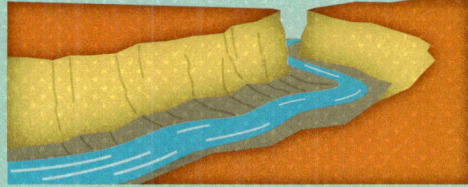

The hard rock collapses.

The waterfall retreats upstream.

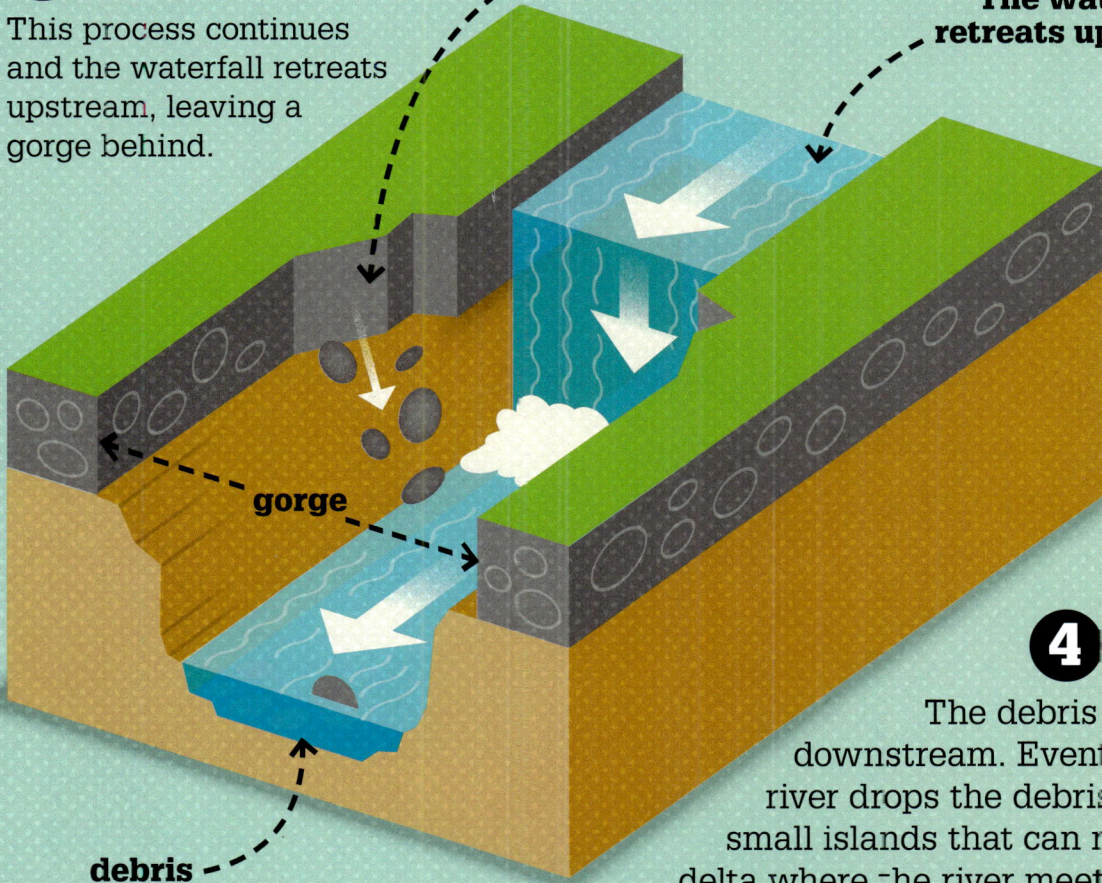

❸ GORGING

This process continues and the waterfall retreats upstream, leaving a gorge behind.

gorge

debris

❹ DELTA

The debris is carried downstream. Eventually, the river drops the debris, forming small islands that can make up a delta where the river meets the sea.

TRY THIS ...

Fill up a tray with wet sand. Support one end of the tray so that it is at an angle. Slowly pour water into the top of the tray and watch as the water flows down, eroding the sand and forming mini-gorges.

21

HOW THE WATER CYCLE WORKS

Over, under and above Earth's surface, water is moving in a continuous cycle. In doing so it changes state, from its liquid form in rivers, seas and lakes, to its gas form as water vapour in the air, or to its solid form as ice in frozen glaciers.

❷ MAKING CLOUDS

Air can only hold so much water vapour. If there is too much water vapour in the air or if the air cools suddenly, the water vapour condenses into droplets. These are small and light enough to stay airborne and form clouds.

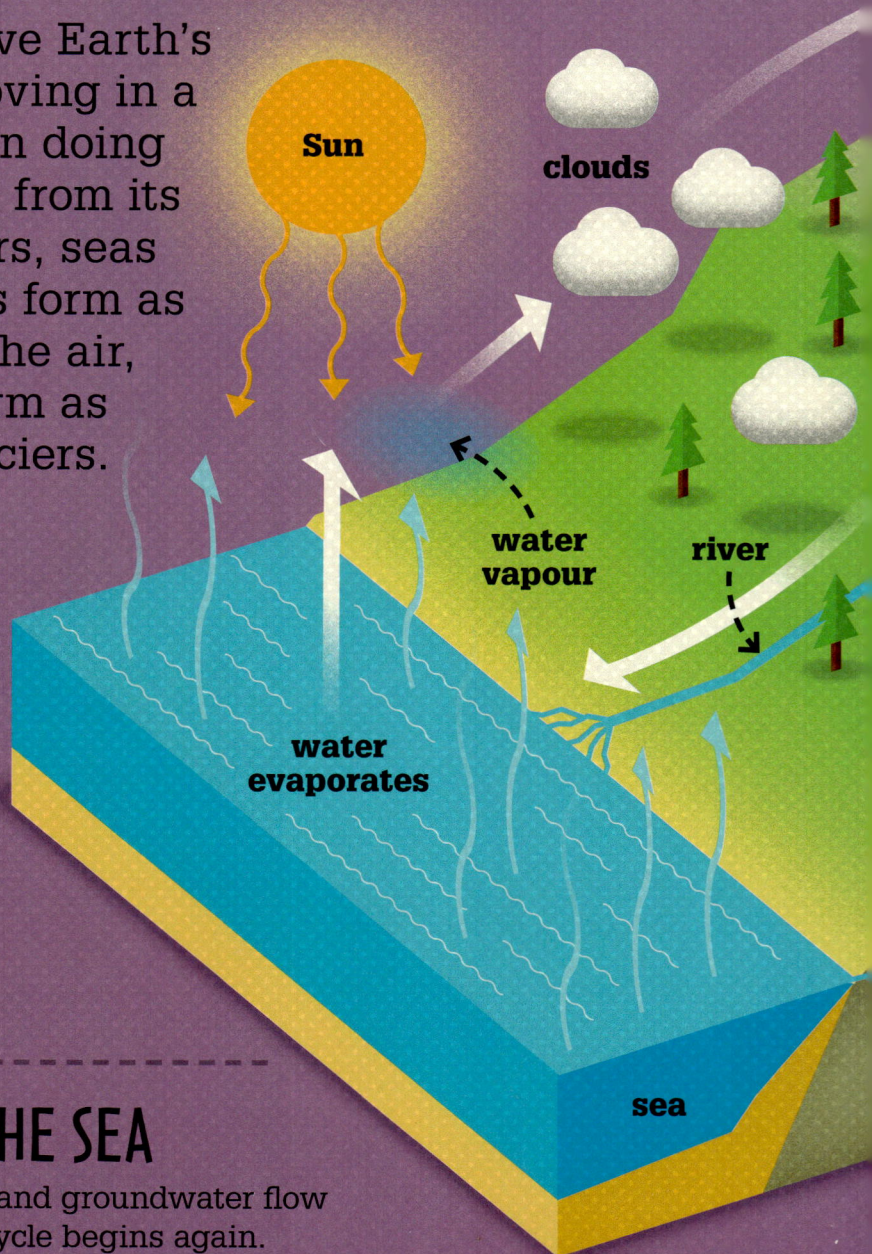

Sun

clouds

water vapour

river

water evaporates

sea

❶ EVAPORATION

As the Sun warms the surface of the sea, water molecules evaporate, becoming gassy water vapour in the air.

❻ BACK TO THE SEA

Eventually, the rivers and groundwater flow into the sea and the cycle begins again.

③ RAIN OR SNOW?

These droplets may fall as rain, or – if it is cold enough – snow. If rain or snow falls on mountain tops or very cold places, then the water may freeze solid as ice and become part of a glacier. This water may not melt again for thousands of years.

TRY THIS ...

Make your own water cycle. Pour two cups of water into a bowl. Stand an empty cup in the bowl and cover it all with cling film. Over a couple of days, water from the bowl will evaporate, condense on the cling film and then fall as 'rain' into the cup.

snow

rain

streams

glacier

rain

groundwater

The greatest amount of rain to fall in a single 24-hour period is 1.825 m on the island of Réunion in the Indian Ocean during tropical cyclone Denise in 1966.

④ MAKING RIVERS

Rain that falls on mountains but doesn't freeze starts to move downhill, collecting together to form streams and rivers.

⑤ GROUNDWATER

Some water seeps into the earth and moves beneath the surface as groundwater.

23

HOW RAIN FALLS

Rain and other types of precipitation, such as snow, form when warm air containing a lot of water vapour cools. The vapour then condenses, forming big drops that fall from the sky.

3 MOUNTAINS

Warm, moist air is pushed up by mountains as it passes over them.

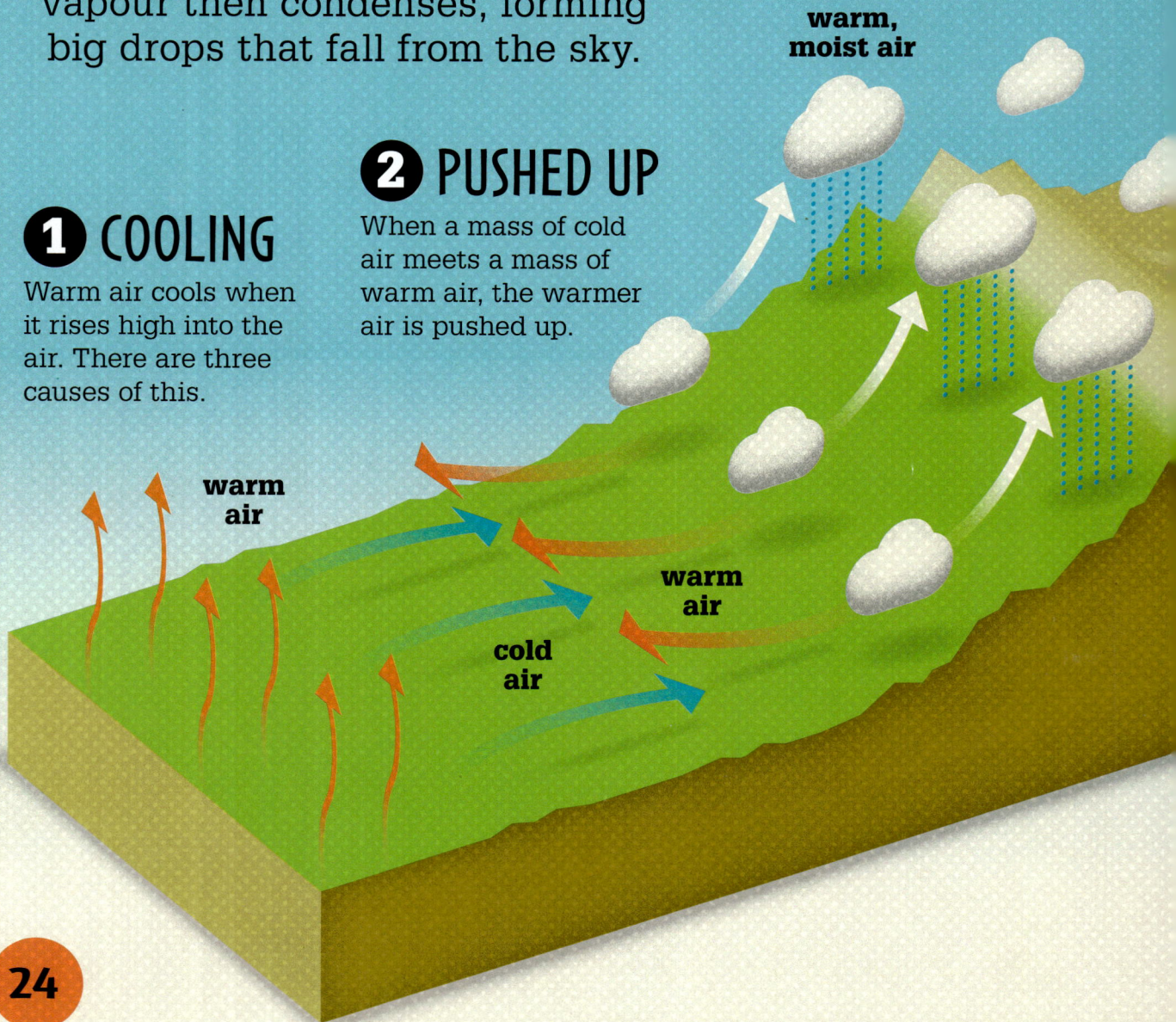

warm, moist air

2 PUSHED UP

When a mass of cold air meets a mass of warm air, the warmer air is pushed up.

1 COOLING

Warm air cools when it rises high into the air. There are three causes of this.

warm air

warm air

cold air

24

4 CONVECTION

When the Sun warms the ground, convection currents form, which carry the warm air up.

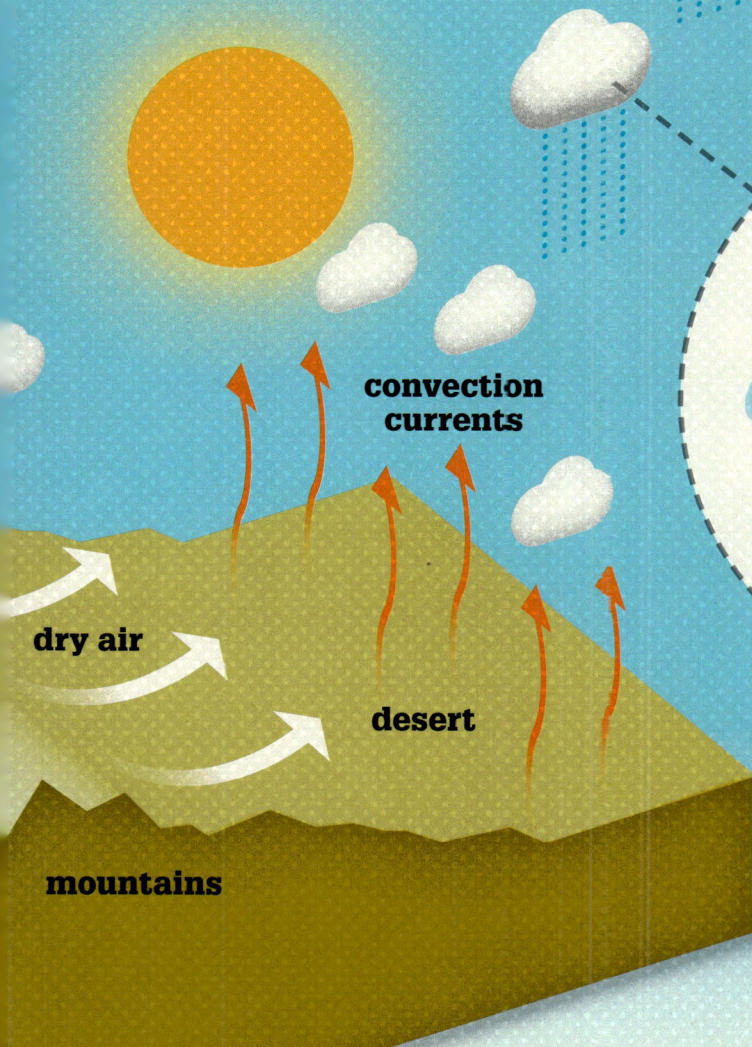

5 FORMING DROPS

Swirling air currents inside the forming clouds cause the water droplets to clump together around dust particles. When they are heavy enough, they fall as rain.

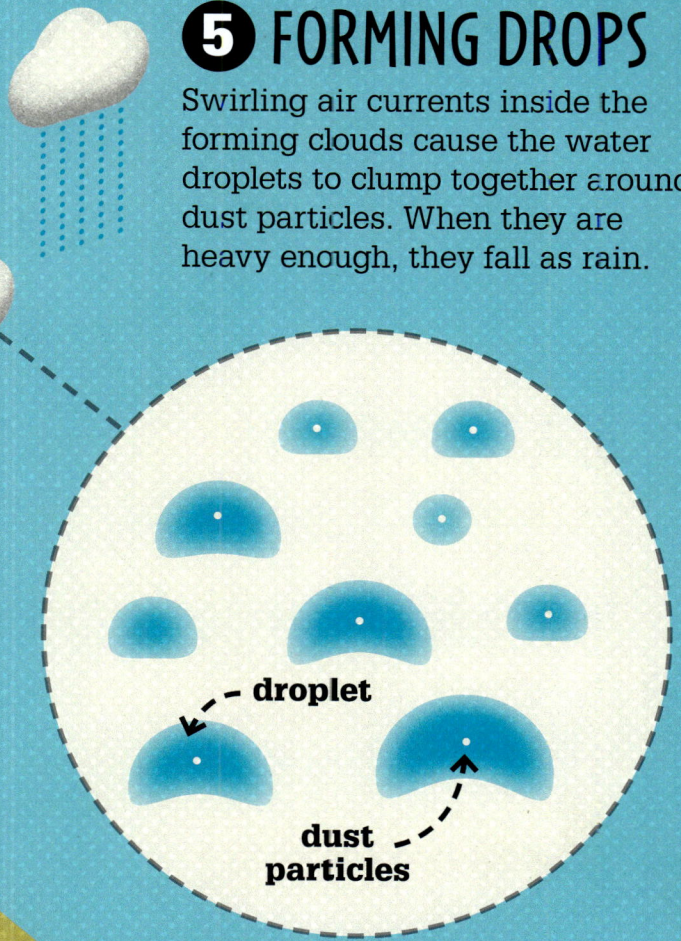

convection currents

dry air

desert

mountains

droplet

dust particles

6 FALLING RAIN

The shape of the raindrops depends on their size. Small droplets are ball-shaped, larger ones become flattened and the biggest are shaped like parachutes.

TRY THIS ...

Make your own rain gauge by asking an adult to cut the top off a plastic bottle. Turn this upside down and put it back in the bottle. Place the bottle outdoors and then use a ruler to measure the amount of rain that falls over a period of time.

HOW
LIGHTNING STRIKES

Powerful forces deep inside storm-clouds build up huge charges of electricity. These are released in sudden, violent flashes of lightning and the crackling rumble of thunder.

❶ STORMS

When storm-clouds form, ice particles inside the clouds are whipped about by strong winds and air currents.

❷ RUBBING

These particles rub against each other, creating a huge build-up of static electricity.

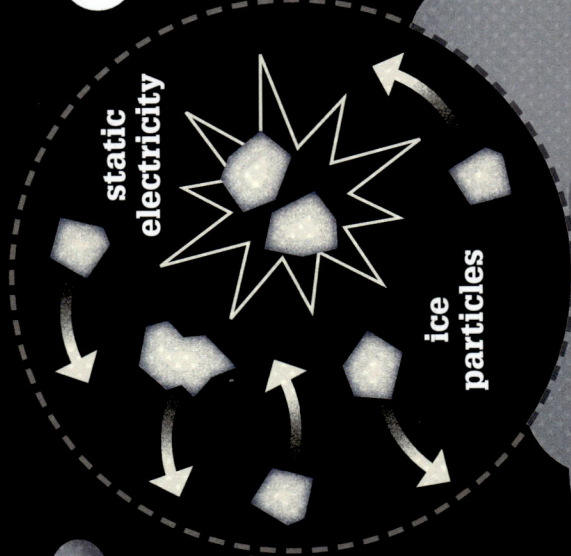

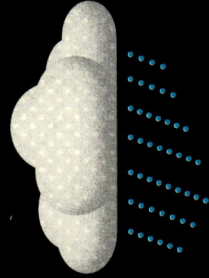

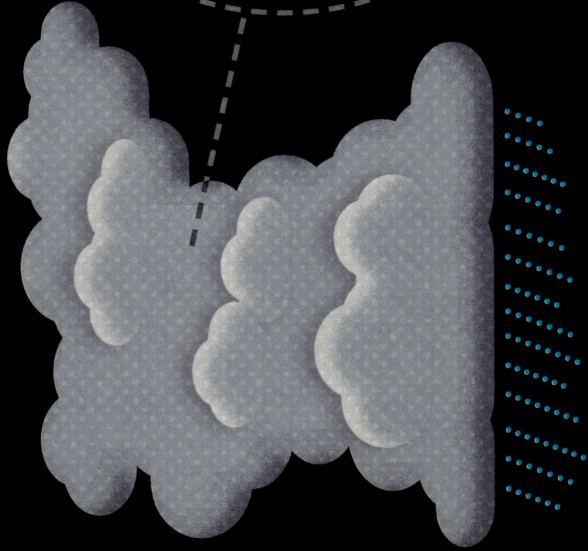

static electricity

ice particles

❸ STATIC BUILD-UP

When enough static charge has built up in the cloud, it is released in a massive flash of lightning.

flash of lightning

❹ LIGHTNING

The lightning flash heats up the air around it so much and so quickly that the air explodes with a loud boom, creating the clash of thunder.

A bolt of lightning has a temperature of 30,000 °C – that's six times hotter than the surface of the Sun! Every second, about 100 lightning bolts strike Earth.

TRY THIS ...

Sound travels 1 km in about 3 seconds. Can you work out how far away a lightning bolt was if you hear the thunder 10.5 seconds after you see the lightning flash?

27

HOW A HURRICANE FORMS

Hurricanes are the most powerful storms on the planet – their swirling clouds can measure hundreds of kilometres across. This type of storm is called a tropical cyclone.

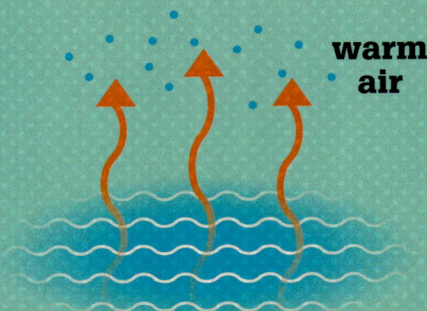

warm air

The cool air sinks.

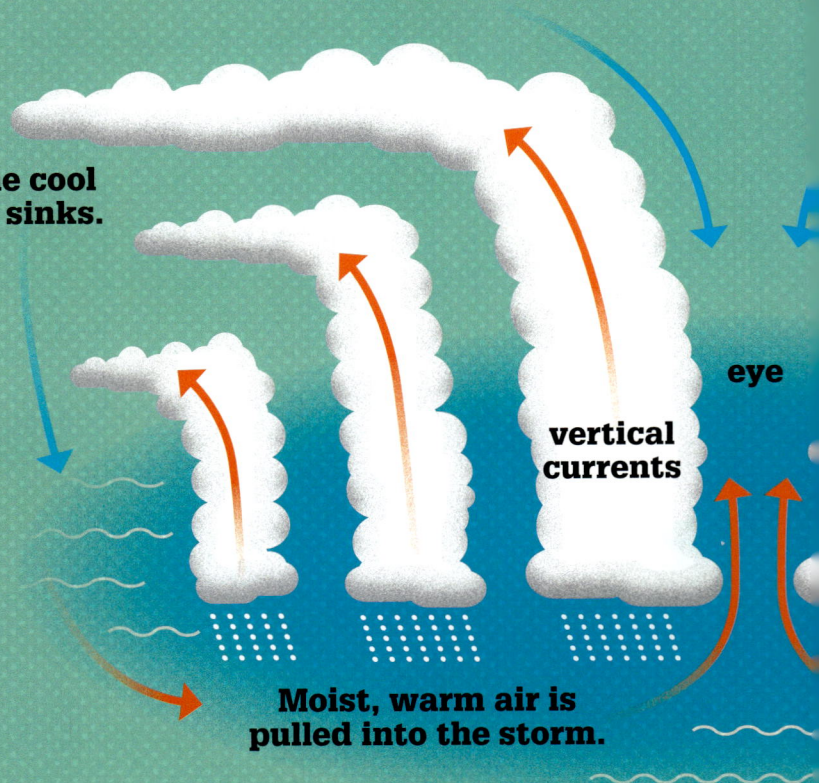

eye

vertical currents

① LOW PRESSURE

Warm air rising over the ocean creates an area of low pressure. This warm air also contains lots of moisture.

cool air

Moist, warm air is pulled into the storm.

② COOLER AIR

Cooler air flows in to replace the warm rising air. This also gets warmer, becomes moist and rises.

③ THUNDER

This process continues, creating huge rain clouds that eventually form thunderstorms.

TRY THIS ...

In the northern hemisphere, tropical cyclones such as hurricanes spin anti-clockwise, while they spin clockwise in the southern hemisphere. Can you find out why?

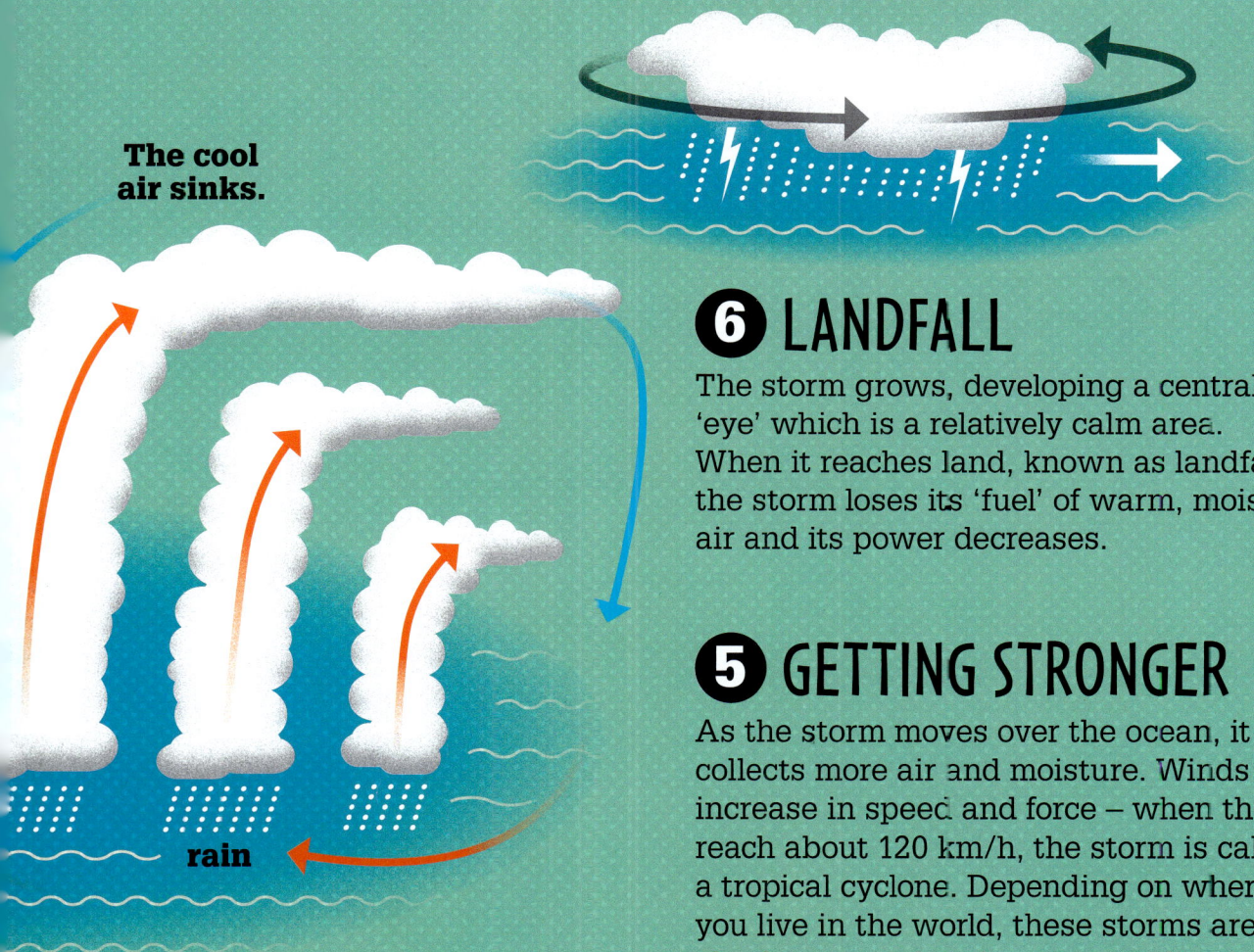

The cool air sinks.

rain

6 LANDFALL

The storm grows, developing a central 'eye' which is a relatively calm area. When it reaches land, known as landfall, the storm loses its 'fuel' of warm, moist air and its power decreases.

5 GETTING STRONGER

As the storm moves over the ocean, it collects more air and moisture. Winds increase in speed and force – when they reach about 120 km/h, the storm is called a tropical cyclone. Depending on where you live in the world, these storms are also known as hurricanes or typhoons.

4 STORM CURRENTS

More and more air is pushed into the storm, creating strong vertical currents. Clouds and winds start to move in a circular motion.

The strength of a hurricane is measured by its category. The most powerful are category 5 hurricanes. They have wind speeds of 250 km/h or more.

29

GLOSSARY

ASTEROID
A small, rocky object in orbit around the Sun.

ATMOSPHERE
A layer of gases surrounding the Earth.

COMET
A small astronomical object made from ice and dust in orbit around the Sun. As it gets close to the Sun, the gas and dust boil off, producing long, glowing tails.

CONDENSE
To change from a gas into a liquid.

CONTINENT
A large body of land on Earth's surface.

CONVECTION CURRENTS
Large circular movements of a fluid as it warms, rises, cools, and then sinks.

CRATER
A large, bowl-shaped hole in the ground that was formed by the impact of a meteorite or comet.

CYCLONE
A large, violent, spinning storm.

DEBRIS
The remains of something that has been broken down.

DELTA
The place where a river meets the sea and deposits large amounts of sediments. This creates small islands and waterways, often in a triangular shape.

EPICENTRE
The place on Earth's surface directly above where an earthquake forms.

ERODE
To wear down rock and carry away the debris.

EVAPORATE
To change from a solid or a liquid state into a vapour.

GAUGE
An instrument that measures the level of something.

GLACIER
A large, thick sheet of ice found around the polar regions or high up on mountains.

GRAVITY
The attractive force that pulls objects with mass towards each other.

GROUNDWATER
Water that seeps into the ground.

HEMISPHERE
Half of a sphere.

ICE CAP
A thick sheet of ice that covers a very large area.

MAGNITUDE

How large or powerful something is.

MANTLE

The part of Earth that lies between the core and the crust. Huge currents of swirling, molten rock push and pull on the crust above causing earthquakes and volcanic eruptions.

MATTER

The physical substance that all things are made of.

METEORITE

A piece of space debris which hits the surface of Earth.

MOLTEN

Softened and turned into a partly liquid state by heat.

OVERHANG

A layer of rock that juts out horizontally over another layer of rock.

PARTICLES

Tiny pieces of matter.

PRECIPITATION

Water that falls from the sky in any form, including rain, snow, sleet and hail.

PROTOPLANETARY DISC

The disc-shaped cloud of dust and rocks around a young star, from which its planets form.

RICHTER SCALE

The scale used to measure the strength or magnitude of earthquakes.

STATIC ELECTRICITY

A type of electrical charge, usually built up by friction.

TECTONIC PLATES

The large plates of rock that make up Earth's crust.

TIDE

The daily rising and falling of the sea level at the coast.

VALLEY

A low-lying area of land between hills or mountains, often with a river running through it.

WEATHERING

To wear down rock into smaller pieces via wind, rain and other weather processes.

ANSWERS...

8-9 You will spot that most earthquakes and volcanoes occur around the edges of tectonic plates.

10-11 It is easier to rub the blocks with the smoother sandpaper against each other because they generate less friction

14-15 The Himalayas will grow by 15,000 mm over the next 2,000 years, which means they will be 15 m taller.

18-19 Neap tides occur twice every orbit of the Moon, when the Moon and Sun are at right angles to Earth. This means there are about 14 days between each neap tide.

26-27 The lightning flash will be 3.5 km away.

28-29 The different direction of rotation is caused by the Coriolis effect. This is a force created by Earth's rotation which pushes air masses to the right in the northern hemisphere and to the left in the southern hemisphere.

INDEX

WEBSITES

www.rockwatch.org.uk
The children's website of the UK's Geologists'
Association, which is a club aimed at inspiring
young people to learn about Earth's processes
and its geology. There's news about events
around the country and a regular magazine.

www.sciencekids.co.nz/geology.html
A fun-packed website with games,
experiments and facts on Earth and
its geology.

FOR MORE AMAZING INFOGRAPHICS, TRY THE FACT-PACKED MAPOGRAPHICA SERIES.

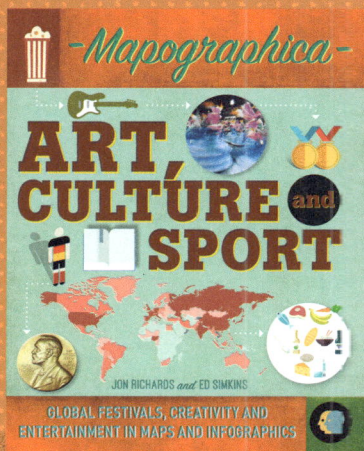

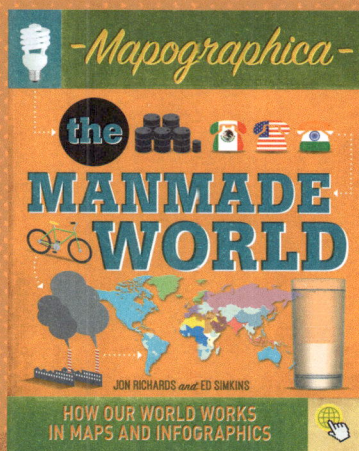

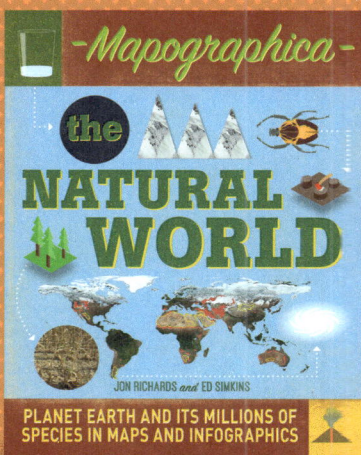

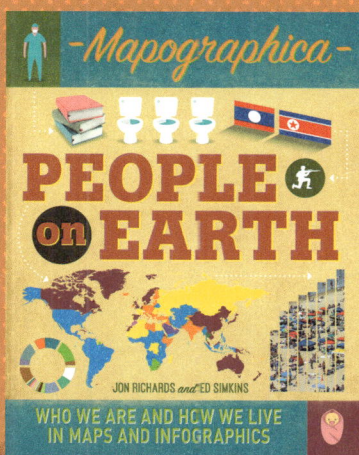